A Rain Washed Notebook

Daniel Richardson

Contents

A Rain Washed Poet	4
Clocking on at the Sawmill	5
The Patron Saint of Lost Things	6
Music from the Desert	8
How did he do that?	9
Red Hair and First Love	10
First Thing Monday Morning	12
Red Mullet	14
The Powerful Charm of Detachment	16
The Innocent Acrobat at the Café	17
A Talkative Saint who Lived in a Hedge	18
Morrab Library Again	20
Leftovers in Berkeley	22
Collapse	24
Not Solving Mathematical Problems on Brandon Hill	25
My Flea Circus	26

A Short History of Treatment for Mental Health Problems in California	27
Kropotkin at the Bookshop	31
Landscape and Conversation	32
Shiva at the Gym	34
Self Image as Contraption	36
The Electric Fence	37
The Whole Neighbourhood Should have been Condemned Years Ago	38
At the Midnight Hour	40
Flight Notes	42
The General's Mistake	44
Wuhan Apricots	46

A Rain Washed Poet

Drinking black coffee in the courtyard of Greg's cottage
under an umbrella in the rain
there appeared to me
high up in the crow's nest
Allen Ginsberg come back again

and welcome I would say
eloquent
outraged
repetitive
master of illusion

still properly Jewish
still mourning the deluded and addicted USA
and the ruined mind of his old friend.

Clocking on at the Sawmill

After a successful breakfast of flapjacks and black coffee
the Buddhist clocking on at the sawmill
250,000 board feet to cut and trim
the moon still bright in the sky
the sun rising
wearing his big red shirt
and his multicoloured coat of equanimity
understood or misunderstood
what I have not and never could.

He has in his mind the mountains
the towering clouds
I see them too
the wild haired sages dancing
although his own feet are not right in the stiff old boots.
The Horsehead Nebula slowing down, some say,
descending its discordant scales
has not anything at all to say for itself.

The Patron Saint of Lost Things

Saint Anthony of Padua
Full of learning as he was
and overflowing with conviction
preached to the fishes
on the coast near Rimini
and, according to legend,
they and other creatures of the sea
raised their heads above the swirling waters
crowds of them
to listen to him

so eloquent he was
so logical
his sentences threaded with light
following huge gravitational pulls
quoting precedents and
making promises
speaking to them directly

the spotted wrasse
the striped wrasse
the stargazer
the common eel

the cetaceans and dwellers of the abyss
the chambered nautilus

the octopus
the Portuguese man of war
and the moon jelly

so beautiful he was,
inclusive,
grammatically sound and self assertive
his beard flowing in the wind
his mind in flight.

Music from the Desert

In the non-violent and democratic republic of the mind
we will do algebra
and tell stories and drink coffee
we will get mortgages with 0% interest
and the Jewish physician will lie down with the
Palestinian architect.

There will be music from the desert.
We will grow melons and make love.
There will be clean water
and the children will get breakfast.

And all the beasts of the sea will leap and multiply
and call to one another in the tides.

How did he do that?

How do you know when you meet one,
one of the good ones?
The rule is, some people say,
you don't notice anything exactly but
you get a sort of unusual
floating feeling
and carried along feeling
like a leaf on a stream, let's say,
and some sense

of an incursion
of ongoing unreality,
although each thing and event is joined to the next,
but it doesn't really
take the centre of your attention

until a special moment,
hard to define,
but quite definite
just
afterwards
when it's finished

and, let's say, you feel a chill,
you pat for your reassuring wallet
and find you don't
actually, even, any more
possess trousers.

Red Hair and First Love

Sweet Pauline
knew the real Doc Rickets
grew up on a chicken farm
outside of Yuba City
and she had to stand up in a line in Church
with the other kids
and say she was a sinner.
I am not, she thought quite firmly.

And after high school
which possibly she did not finish
when her father came to see her off
on the bus to San Francisco
and (his idea) they said a prayer together,
and he mentioned, once again, that
once you are saved, you are saved forever.
Oh Daddy, she wanted to tell him
(but hadn't the heart)
I never was saved at all.

In the city she started reading
Carson McCullers
Karl Marx,
William Faulkner.

She met a furious minded married Communist
with a nice beard,
worked on the newspaper
got pregnant, couldn't go home again.

She and her son lived in
a house in Monterey
which was, it seemed, held together by its wall
paper.
He cried and cried
with a long lasting fury he might have got from his
beautiful father.

She carried him along Cannery Row
to Pacific Grove
which was a dry town, Methodist,
to the popular liquor store
on the boundary
telling him about the
contradictory and interesting world
polyps and anemones
Democratic politics
and flocking birds and fishes,
trying to explain the civilizing thing
which is hard to use
and beyond price.

First Thing Monday Morning

She turned the manikin around
so that it was facing into the shop and
had its back to the street.
It was wearing khaki coloured trousers
and a blue shirt with the sleeves rolled up
looking ready to do something.

She knelt down and
reached up into its trousers right leg
and pulled and pulled
something out.
Was she undoing a foot or an ankle?
Then there wasn't a right leg at all
so it was standing, it seemed,
just on its left leg
and then she unrolled and unbuttoned its cuffs,
then unbuttoned down the front of its blouse
so that its yellowy
bare back was showing.

Then she took off its head
and put it to one side.
It was still a manikin although with no head
and wearing trousers
although without a right leg
but then she lifted off its body
so that it seemed to be just empty trousers
standing up.

She pulled the trousers up and off
which you can not do normally
and there wasn't anything left but a metal pole
which, maybe, stood on three
curved legs, like a hat stand.

She was sort of thoughtful
about it all the time
not absent minded at all
not too fast,
not too slow.

Red Mullet

First they said that everyone
although it might be impossible for us to understand,
our understanding being limited,
and we agree that our understanding is limited
and has always been limited
got what was coming to them,
yes
or they would get it eventually.
Green wrass and spotted wrass.
Anemone.
Portuguese man of war.

And then they said that everyone,
possibly by hard work,
listen to this now
and not being discouraged, no matter what happened,
could get what they really wanted.
Sand, kelp, blue plastic.
Wet granite,
little sea bird.

And then they said,
ha, ha,
sea urchin and chambered nautilus
that you have in fact chosen,
although part of the way it works
is that you may not be able to admit it,
no, you may not,
the life
sand worms
and the encircling water
and little sea bird on quick legs
which you do in fact have.

The Powerful Charm of Detachment

Clementine was reading
sitting in the flowered armchair by the window.
Her son was doing something
with toy cars and tanks on the floor.

Occasionally he would make faint blowing up
noises.
Sounds would come from his vicinity
of distant shouting,
howled instructions,
denials, arrangements.

She was beautiful and detached while reading,
and when she paused and looked up
she was unfaltering in her regard.
And meanwhile he was absorbed
in moment to moment
struggles of desperate imaginary men
who were as temporary and insubstantial
as shadows or spots of sun
and who had plenty to say for themselves
but not enough time to say it
before they were
betrayed, insulted, and
cruelly destroyed.

The Innocent Acrobat at the Café

The angular remorseless acrobatic girl
with her papers in front of her at the wooden table
mostly crossed out
wraps her legs around each other
leans forward
scowls sometimes
open faced flying girl
yes, I said, yes, flying
in her blue and white striped shirt
not letting go
and going reddish in her forehead and over her neck
and then leaning back with the heels of her hands behind her ears,
considering her options.

The mistakes and the wrong ideas
are getting what they have coming to them
and they are rapidly slinking away
from her terrifying even handedness
and sometimes
looking back at her
ashamed of themselves
but still looking back
over their shoulders

A Talkative Saint who Lived in a Hedge

He was caught up in what he did
and he couldn't do enough of it
and he did it all the time.

He would talk about it to anyone
even if they told him they couldn't understand a word
of it
and didn't want to listen
and he wouldn't stop.
He would run after you to tell you
that the thing he told you yesterday
although not incorrect
was not what he meant at the time.

Walking from Penzance to Newlyn,
to buy a fish or two,
it would be quicker some people said to go by Lamorna,
avoiding him in his place in the hedge.

He was not St. Cuby.
He was not St. Caradoc.
And he was not St. Erth.

Where he came from:
some say he paddled over from Ireland
in a wooden washtub
with the purpose of getting away from himself.
But he would tell you

even if that was a true story
it was about someone else.

People missed him when he was gone.
They would now and then stop
by his place in the hedge
and wait for a while,
as if they expected something,
even fairly sensible people.

Morrab Library Again

A slippage of time might become an avalanche.
I hold fast to the greasy ropes
and what I have reckoned by the swaying light
Morrab library Penzance
in the Celtic Sea
longitude 5 degrees 30' 13.74" West
with some margin for error.

Among the circling and intersecting paths
ferns and palm trees
smudged calculations
in the swaying watery light
from measurements made
with corroded instruments
I hear the voices of men and women.

It is said that if there is such a thing as another life
there might be or there must be
or there must have been
an exact replica
of the Morrab library
and there or here
it is possible to read old murder mysteries
or Lord Nelson's dispatches
or George Mackay Brown.

I look out the high windows of the library and
briefly observe
although I do not hear his footsteps on the gravel
a lookalike of Alfred Wallis
fisherman of the toothed and wayward North
Atlantic sea
and husband to a woman 20 years his senior
carrying scraps of wood and metal
as he would be on his way to do
what he only did because he loved it,
another painting.

Leftovers in Berkeley

The woman, poor and hard working,
 lives on almost nothing.
She does not speak.
Her hands are dirty and swollen.
Carrying her plastic bag,
she comes out from the bushes behind the institute
and climbs the wooden stairs to the deck.
She does not admit that you can see her.
Like a raccoon in the daylight.
Her posture, her movements, her eyes, her hands
deny her visibility.

She threads her way around
the tables and the standing groups
of persistent minded scholars,
mostly men but some women,
having their lunch,
visitors and relative strangers

from the other ends of the world,
talking as well as they can
of abstract things,
fantastic sea creatures of ideas,
in a deft patchwork of languages,
English, Spanish, Russian, French.

Even if you knew her
you could not speak to her.
She collects from the bin
unfinished watermelon, roast beef sandwich,

some Caesar salad, a discarded chicken leg,
a ripe peach
into her bag
and goes again down the stairs
and out into the dry hills
which are as old as Ethiopia.

Collapse

The ruins of beautiful intentions
are on the table,
devastated,
opened out, spread out
following
cellular knowledge of light
which is not really mistaken
a parachute of frilled leaves
a trace of unearthly purple,
anemones.

Not Solving Mathematical Problems on Brandon Hill

With after effects of the virus,
recovering maybe,
a little dizzy,
I try counting the crows
but they keep changing places
and giving me funny looks
lurching and staggering
in their feather pantaloons
bending backwards their knees, or possibly heels
until their kaleidoscopic intentions and impulses
cohere, enknott, coagulate,
close accounts and,

taking on competence in full
they swoop very low over the grass
over the manoeuvring, ramified shadows,
which I don't have the time to pay attention to,
and up into the spacious, concealing trees.

My Flea Circus

Came in a cardboard box
not the same as a shoebox
but flatter, shorter, wider,
quite a long time ago,
worn cardboard
cloud coloured blue or brown or yellow off white
I don't know if it worked or not.
Some of it got lost
or worn out or broken.
I have the small trapeze,
I am sitting on the drum
and I see underneath my street clothes
the ragged and twisted remnants
of my red costume.

A Short History of Treatment for Mental Health Problems in California

There were not many crazy people
in San Francisco in the early days
and some of them were discreet and kept their heads down
but there were some
who were, or were liable to be,
taken to an old ship called the Elphemia
anchored not quite level in the bay
which had holes in the deck
so that now and then
a maniac or a possible maniac would fall into the bilge,
which was quite deep,
since it needed regular pumping out
to counteract the steady leaking
and so required more discipline than was available

because for one thing
people kept coming and going
some talking their way out and starting a new life under a different name,
and some never having been crazy anyway,
not even slightly,
and some unaccounted for,
one or two jumping over the side,
and swimming for normal life on the shore,
and also there were distractions,

visitors being allowed,
or not noticed,
small boats coming and going at all hours,
and according to rumours
drinking,
gambling,
nudity,
a lack of hygiene,
disease,
prostitution,
money changing hands,
all to some extent visible by binoculars from the shore
or in imagination

so and therefore
they moved all these people to Agnew's farm
out in lettuce growing Santa Clara county,
home of the rain king sprinkler,
where not many would go for a good time
and there they had a severe regime
with doctors and ill paid nurses,
cold showers and restraints,

until, due to the nearby branch of the San Andreas fault,
the great earthquake of 1906
collapsed the stone buildings
in which there were now lots of crazy people
killing many
although, it is said, some lunatics and catatonics
discovering almost superhuman strength
broke their shackles
or pulled them out of the collapsing walls
and some, hairy and partly naked though they might be,
did heroic deeds,
rescuing other inmates and doctors and orderlies,
some escaping in borrowed clothes,
and some sort of waiting or detained

until it started up again with more energy
with a motto of cheerfulness
in new buildings with modern ideas, albeit crude,
better qualified staff
and there they did eventually in the treatment tower
lobotomies, leucotomies
some of them quick ones going in through the eyes
with an instrument similar to an ice pick
and shock treatments on a large scale
and in the vogue for what they called eugenics
many enforced sterilizations,
applications of Largactil,
expanding and developing over the years
emitting reptilian papers with many authors,
including statistical analysis
justifying everything,

until Ronald Reagan closed it down,
partly to save money,
along with most of the other state mental hospitals,
so that now
most of the crazy people
if not in prison
are wandering around, where they may or may not belong,
with the rest of us
some of us more or less crazy ourselves,
who knows?
going about our business
as well as we can
in the smeared and spoiled
glaring coercive ordinariness of California.

Kropotkin at the bookshop

I met my friend Peter Kropotkin
at the bookshop in Rope Walk
off Gaol Ferry Road.
His face was streaked with tears.

We didn't speak about the news this morning.
I knew his wife was born in Kyiv.
The bookshop glowed.
In the middle of the central table
his most famous book was displayed.

My eyes were opened
when I went to Siberia, he said.
I was immersed in the ideas of Darwin.
I expected to see a savage competition within species
the survival, you know, of the fittest
and what I saw
the horses in the wind and snow and ice
forming a circle when attacked by wolves.
There was no place at all for competition
in that harsh world.

Landscape and Conversation

Process and practice if you like
and another thing that might
come out of this I think…
She has a big mouth, big bones, broad hips
and there is
a wrinkled darkness over her face
as she speaks.

Across from her, the
thinner woman does not cease or flag
in her attention,
but glances back and forth between
the face and eyes of the speaker and her own
notebook,

meanwhile the top of her pencil
vibrates, wavers, pauses
and vibrates again,
recording the main points
of the slew and avalanche
and herding
and coalescence

of mists and rocks and roots and
clouds and long legged
beasts with horns
in their ancient
paths of migration,
not to speak of the little
dishes of steaming porridge

left out
along the way,
as the more powerful woman
expresses
a few very tentative
and preliminary ideas and opinions.

Shiva at the Gym

He is sitting on a static bicycle,
peddling steadily, moving on,
and reading the N.Y. Times
which is spread out on the handlebars in front of
him,
and listening to something
I suppose music.

He has that mild worn out
N.Y. face
which contains a map of the
sadness of competition
and sex and sexual organs
so precious and wrinkled
inflatable to some extent.

Across the dried deltas of cracked clay
grey and brown and white
he pedals
around the marshes
and the margins of villages and isolated houses
around the dogs and the flies
and the smoke of fires.
He slowly mounts a bank
and the green of the patchy grass
washes over him.
At the top
white and grey and cracked earth
brown mottles
and spreads over his skin and

his mouth breaks into sky
blue fragments
and he breathes in and out
the flowering sun.

Self Image as Contraption

Curving stalk interlocked
adam's apple
supporting skull
calavera
with its ears and eyes
aspects and focus
colours and glissandos
and scrapings and tic toc
holding in the folded brain
map and forest and seaweed
and mistakes and tides and hormonal surges
no traffic rules at all
and little fish going about their business
in the glimmering shadows.

The musical rib cage
and stubborn feet
cock and balls
perfidious and unreliable
have their own single mindedness and history
which may not make a lot of sense
to the assemblage and bricolage
or the quorum
or the rest of the pulsing, bubbling
rattletrap, fermenting federation contraption.

The Electric Fence

The bull worse than ever
they turned up the power.
So when Shorty pissed on the electric fence
it blew him right over the hedge
heaven and earth bass-ackwards
and landed almost on top of the bull in
consequence
which butted him and skittered him,
his trousers still smoking,
into the slurry pit
which burst into flame.

When I visited him in hospital
he was almost unrecognizable.

Why does this stuff always happen to me? He
complained.

The bull, however, had been entertained
and eagerly hoped to meet soon again:
same characters, very same plot.
Better than sex, he might have thought
had he a more reflective brain.

The Whole Neighbourhood Should Have Been Condemned Years Ago

They'd got the new beautiful lead valley in
and put the old tiles back on as the sky darkened
and laid out a strip of black plastic on the top of
the valley roof
the damp course to be, and arranged the coping
stones on top.

And Jay and Louise made love in the valley
they were so happy with it
although in general she preferred a bed
and he was almost more in love with the lead
which might last 500 years
and was so perfect and inert
the dull suaveness of it.

They planned to cement it in the morning
but in the morning the storm and the erratic wind
came to Totterdown
out of wild Siberia
houses collapsed
whose main beams were more rotten than usual
cats were blown into hedges and
rubbish bins took themselves down the street
skittering.

Jay looked out and saw an old lady almost flying
against her will
and then they heard a terrible
intimate
grating grinding sound
like a giant wisdom tooth being pulled
and a horrible continuing sliding crash.

You aren't going up there she said
in her practical voice
but he was already out the kitchen door
in the fury and the roaring and the flying grit
ascending the wobbly ladder to the roof.

Yes, don't worry, he called,
it will be alright.
Damn you, she yelled,
you always say that.

At the midnight hour

He had been convicted of fraud to do with
benefits.
They said that he was working while claiming to
be unemployed.
And also claiming to be at least two people at the
same time.
And if he wasn't doing that he was part of a
conspiracy
so complicated it wasn't worth the trouble to
untangle.
Just one look at him and you could see he was
illegal.

She was thin and secretive, and
looked at everyone sideways with her dark eyes.
She wore fraying tights and scuffed shoes.
She thought maybe
she only thought he was more doomed
than other people because she knew him better.

There weren't any doubts about it however:
they had such good times together.
No one but him it seemed knew
that when she shucked off her clothes
she was like an angel from paradise.

Don't worry, he said.
He said that a lot.
He said everything was OK really.
It didn't make a big dent in her feelings
but she appreciated his mentioning his opinion.
He changed his name and dyed his hair.
Her complaint was that he was not
straightforward
and not practical
and got caught.
His was that she did not respect him
and that she was so often depressed.

Gorgeous and holding roses absent mindedly
at the midnight hour
they sail under the moon
and over the V shaped roofs of Totterdown.

Flight Notes

The octogenarian aeronaut
showed me his leather helmet
and let me try it on
and his flying suit
and said that he was uncertain
or even less than that
if such were logically possible
as to where or when he had attempted
what you might call flight
if that word could be used about it
in what twilight
or warm and foggy night
under what craggy moon
not to speak of the wind conditions
and the forked lightning
and the hailstones
he had attempted it.

He had not met Teresa of Avila or the Queen
or Mohammad on his horse
or other famous levitationers
in the realms of cumulo-nimbus
but had once encountered
landing or crashing next to
a sensible and welcoming Italian lady on a
haystack
who had been moon viewing.

It was like falling he said
overwhelming and uncontrollable
but less alarming.

I am neither for it
nor against it
if it exists at all.
It is not bad as far as it goes, he allowed.
It is not a thing which happens
when you try to make it happen
nor is it a thing which ceases
when you or someone else wishes it to cease.

The General's Mistake

All the curtains were drawn
in the streets of Poznan.
The people followed instructions to the letter
But not a lot of work was done.

The ancient Graffin
as wise as the sphinx
danced close to the Graf
in her Chanel 5, her pearls and her mink.

The coughing of tanks on parade,
the guns dripping with flowers,
the creaking of treads,
the non-stop trombones mixed with
the interminable squeaking of beds.

They knew
what to do
and more than once
in Ustka and Puck
and weren't far behind
in Sopit and Skupsk.
They weren't so lucky in Piovki
and did as well as they could
in Lublin and Bialystok.

If it wasn't exactly like that I'm sorry
But at least I believe I read in the paper that
Marital law in Poland had been decreed.
And compliance, with the strictest formality,
whether or not you agreed,
must be the new normality.

And even if it was a mistake
we could see,
whether or not it was legally required,
what had always been
and was now really desired.

Wuhan Apricots

Wei Lin was a professor
of geometric logic at Wuhan University.
Everybody loved him
because of the clarity of his mind
and because of his democratic courtesy.
He was a little bit famous in China
and his name was spoken also,
so it was said,
by scholars
even in Russia and in the United States
or at least it was spoken the last time,
not recently to tell the truth,
anyone who understood this obscure subject
got out and came back again.
If you looked in the door of his office
there he would be
writing lines of symbols
or drawing diagrams.
But whatever he was doing
he would stop to talk.
Thought can not be interrupted, he said.
How encouraging!

However, in connection with many other events of that time,
he was accused, by a certain ad hoc committee,
of worshiping foreign ideas.
He replied that he worked
in an ancient and international tradition.
He was accused of licking the arseholes
of imperialist Americans and or revisionist Russians,
and of habitually doing other even less attractive actions.

He replied, with nervous dignity,
that, objectively speaking, the foremost
practitioners in his field
lived either in New York city or in Moscow.

He was accused of elitist essentialism
and of ignoring the concrete realities
of the socialist struggle.

And then, recognising the seriousness of this,
and the aspects of truth in it,
he admitted his faults
and said that he would reform himself
with the aid of the correct ideas of Mao Tse Tung
and the useful criticism of his comrades.
And in this way he got off, you might say, easy.

Then his wife died.
She fell over dead in the kitchen.
He loved her so much.
She was the rainbow,
and the habit of his life.
She was his old friend.
He collapsed into himself.
He came to work most days,
and continued his scholarship as well as he could.
If you looked into his office
he would be bent over his papers,
but sometimes his face was streaked with tears.

During that summer, Wuhan was, as usual, hot and humid,
and at the university there was chaos and disorder, fighting
between the red guards and the 100,000 heroes
shooting at each other with machine guns,
and busily digging trenches and tunnels.

Wei Lin with other things in mind,
made his way down by the fish market
and took a certain bus
and then a ferry over the river
and then another bus out into the flat country
to buy apricots or asparagus.
He and the grandmother of the apricot girl
would usually sit on boxes out there under the
walnut trees
where there was an acrid persisting smell of green
walnuts
and a sweet smell of ripe or over ripe apricots
and, while the girl quietly listened to them,
they joked and talked in dialect,
about many things,
with so many double meanings,
one inside the other,
in that conversation they held in that dusty court,
that if you wrote it down
and took it home
and studied it for a year,
it would make you dizzy and
you still could not understand it all.
Then he always went up the stairs
with the apricot girl.
The sun shone through the shutters.
Their hearts pounded
and, in spite of everything,
they made what seemed to be the best love of the
world in that place.

Then one day he fell off the bus and broke his leg.
In his distress, and following his remarkable belief in honesty,
he tried to explain what had happened.
As part of his effort to straighten everything out,
he told his daughter he wanted to marry the apricot girl.
She denounced him immediately.
He was firmly invited by the committee
to return for more discussion.
It was said that a person with nothing to hide
would have nothing to fear,
and he was accused

- of foolishness
- of dishonesty
- of lack of openness
- of exploitation of the youth
- of abuse of his position
- of dishonouring the memory of his wife, only recently buried
- of dishonouring his daughter
- of lewd and unseemly behaviour in the countryside
- of exploitation of the peasants
- of ignoring the previous advice given to him
- of incorrect accounting for his time
- of essentialist philosophy
- of ignoring the concrete realities of the Socialist struggle
- of misleading the students
- of delusions of grandeur
- of holding mistaken ideas against reason

- of consorting with a known prostitute
- of refusing to admit his faults

Eighteen faults, it was said.
What does such a person deserve?
Seven beatings for each fault.
How many is that?

In this way it happened that he had to wear a tall
pointed hat.
which said: False Authority.
He was beaten, on several occasions, and
his books were kicked and torn.
He was made to piss on them.
These are only books, he said, and I may have
made mistakes,
but the ideas are immortal.
This line of thought was not considered to be
sound.
It may be true after all, he admitted eventually
that logic originated in China.
And that all of this is necessary.
And that logic itself is not of primary importance
compared to correct politics.
He respectfully requested to resign
and to re-educate himself among the peasantry,
both of which he was actually required to do.

Up a ladder,
hands and feet sometimes uncertain,
but mind clear, relatively speaking,
wearing a straw hat against the sun
Wei Lin would stop sometimes to think.
and even take out a little notebook
and write in it,
a line of symbols
or a diagram.

Nothing ever finished in here,
he said,
of his head,
of his heart,
of his manhood,
of his notebook.
You pay attention! the boss yelled at him.
Pick faster!

Acknowledgements

I would like to say thank you to the editors of the following publications in which some of these poems first appeared.

Dream Catcher: The Patron Saint of Lost Things, At the Midnight Hour

Dreich: Flight Notes, The General's Mistake

Ink Sweat and Tears: Clocking on at the Sawmill, Red Mullet, A Talkative Saint who lived in a hedge, How did he do that?

Obsessed with Pipework: First Thing Monday Morning, The Innocent Acrobat at the Cafe

Raceme: The Whole Neighbourhood should have been Condemned Years ago

Rhinoceros (from Stairwell Books): Wuhan Apricots

Thanks also for conversation, advice and encouragement from the members of the *Leaping Word Poetry Consultancy.*

Daniel Richardson

RSVP

d.s.richardsonxx@gmail.com

Printed in Great Britain
by Amazon